Animal Friends

Projects and Activities for Grades K-3

Written by Denise Bieniek

Illustrated by Laura Ferraro

10 9 8 7 6 5 4 3

Copyright © 1996 by Troll Communications L.L.C. All rights reserved. Permission is hereby granted to the purchaser to reproduce these pages, in sufficient quantities to meet yearly student needs, for use in the buyer's classroom. All other permissions must be obtained from the publisher.

Troll Early Learning Activities

Troll Early Learning Activities is a classroom-tested series designed to provide time-pressured teachers with a wide range of theme-related projects and activities to enhance lesson plans and enrich the curriculum. Each book focuses on a different area of early childhood learning, from math and writing to art and science. Using a wide range of activities, each title in this series is chockful of innovative ideas, handy reproducible pages, puzzles and games, classroom projects, suggestions for bulletin boards and learning centers, and much more.

With highly interactive student projects and teacher suggestions that make learning fun, Troll Early Learning Activities is an invaluable classroom resource you'll turn to again and again. We hope you will enjoy using the worksheets and activities presented in these books. And we know your students will benefit from the dynamic, creative learning environment you have created!

Titles in this series:

Animal Friends: Projects and Activities for Grades K-3

Circle Time Fun: Projects and Activities for Grades Pre-K-2

Classroom Decorations: Ideas for a Creative Classroom

Early Literacy Skills: Projects and Activities for Grades K-3

Helping Hands: Small Motor Skills Projects and Activities

Hi, Neighbor! Projects and Activities About Our Community

Number Skills: Math Projects and Activities for Grades K-3

People of the World: Multicultural Projects and Activities

Our World: Science Projects and Activities for Grades K-3

Seasons and Holidays: Celebrations All Year Long

Story Time: Skill-Building Projects and Activities for Grades K-3

Time, Money, Measurement: Projects and Activities Across the Curriculum

---

Metric Conversion Chart

1 inch = 2.54 cm	1 foot = .305 m	1 yard = .914 m
1 mile = 1.61 km	1 fluid ounce = 29.573 ml	1 cup = .24 l
1 pint = .473 l	1 teaspoon = 4.93 ml	1 tablespoon = 14.78 ml

Contents

Fishy Contractions

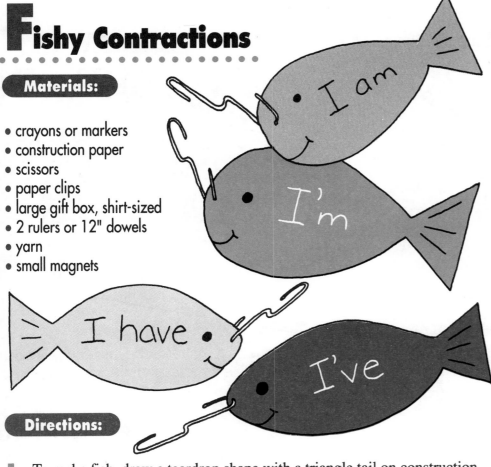

Materials:

- crayons or markers
- construction paper
- scissors
- paper clips
- large gift box, shirt-sized
- 2 rulers or 12" dowels
- yarn
- small magnets

Directions:

1. To make fish, draw a teardrop shape with a triangle tail on construction paper and cut out. You may wish to alter the teardrop shape to create round, fat, flat, long, and skinny fish. Children may add features such as eyes and mouth to the fish.

2. Unfold a paper clip and poke it through the front of one fish, as shown. Repeat for the remaining fish.

3. On one of the fish, write a subject-verb combination; on another fish, write its contraction. Some suggestions are: I have—I've, she does not—she doesn't, they are—they're, you would—you'd, you will—you'll, we cannot—we can't, I am—I'm, it is—it's, and he should not—he shouldn't. Think up more with the class.

4. Make two ponds by coloring the inside of each half of a large gift box blue. Place the subject-verb combination fish in one of the box halves and the contraction fish in the other half.

5. To make the fishing poles, tie one end of a 20" length of yarn to the end of a ruler and the other end to a small magnet. (Round magnets with a hole in the center work best.)

6. Children may fish by trying to catch a fish from one pond and catch the matching contraction fish from the other pond. If the two fish do not match, the player must throw them back and gets one more chance; if they do match, the next player goes. The player with the most matches wins.

7. Store all the parts for this game inside the gift box. Decorate the outside so children may locate the game on their own.

© 1996 Troll Early Learning Activities

Feely Box

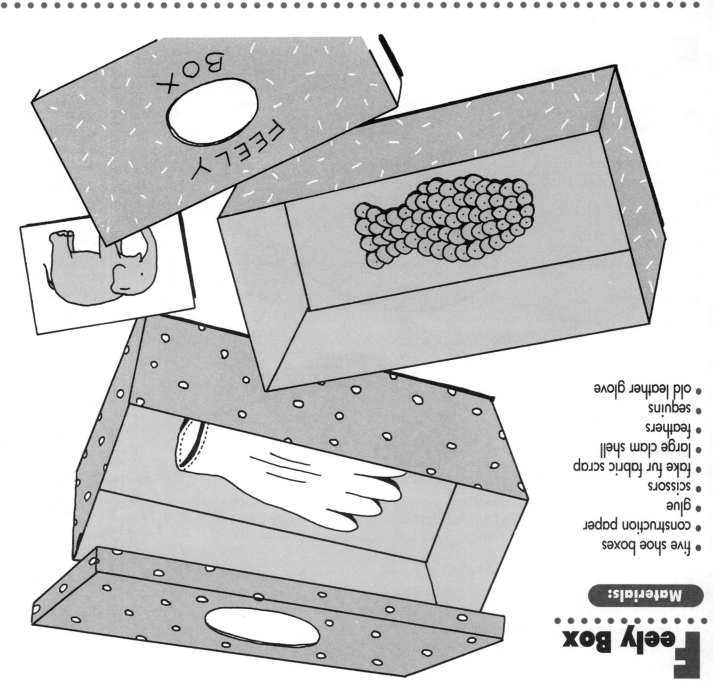

© 1996 Troll Early Learning Activities

Materials:

- five shoe boxes
- construction paper
- scissors
- glue
- fake fur fabric scrap
- large clam shell
- feathers
- sequins
- old leather glove

Directions:

1. Reproduce the animal pictures on page 7 twice. Color and cut them out.

2. To make the feely boxes, cover each shoe box with different, brightly colored construction paper. Cover the boxes and lids separately.

3. Cut a hole large enough for a child's hand to fit through in each box top.

4. Glue a piece of fake fur to the bottom of the first box. Make the piece large enough so children can feel it easily. In the second box, glue around the rim of a large clam shell and place it on the inside bottom. Glue feathers to the inside bottom of the third box. Arrange and glue sequins in a fish shape to the inside bottom of the fourth box. Begin at one end and progress to the opposite side so the "scales" will be layered, as shown. Finally, place an old leather glove in the last box.

5. Glue the animal that is represented inside the box on an interior panel of each box. Lay the other set of animal pictures near the boxes.

6. Ask a volunteer to put his or her hand inside each box, then place the picture of the appropriate animal on top. To self-check, students may look inside the boxes when finished to see if the animals match.

Feely Box

© 1996 Troll Early Learning Activities

Animal Rhyme Box

Materials:

- large box (i.e., photocopy-paper box)
- construction paper
- crayons or markers
- toy animals
- objects that rhyme with the animal names
- oaktag

goat/boat

hen/pen

hat/cat

Directions:

1. Wrap the outside of an empty box with construction paper. Draw pictures of animals on the outside to decorate the box.

2. Ask students to gather together all the toy animals they can find in the classroom. If animals are scarce, you may wish to write a letter home asking to borrow some of the children's toy animals, or borrow them from another classroom.

3. Display these animals on a table. Discuss the name of each one. Then ask the class to think of rhymes for each animal's name.

4. On a large piece of oaktag, write down as many rhymes as possible in columns so children can see the rhyming groups.

5. Rummage through the classroom to find one object from each rhyming group. When an animal has been rhymed, place it and its rhyming match into the box.

6. Then play a rhyming game with the class. Hold up an animal and ask a volunteer to say its name. Then hold up two or three objects (one of which rhymes with the animal's name) and ask which objects rhyme with the name of the animal.

7. After students become familiar with the game, place it on a shelf or on a table for children to play with during free time.

Habitat Wheel

Materials:

- crayons or markers
- scissors
- large sheet of oaktag
- glue
- clothespins (type that open and shut)
- folder with pockets

Directions:

1. Reproduce the animal habitats and animal pictures on pages 10 and 11. Color the pictures and cut them out.

2. Mount the animal pictures onto oaktag. Glue each picture to one side of a clothespin with the top of the picture facing the open end, as shown.

3. To make the wheel, cut an oaktag circle with a 12" diameter. Divide the circle into 8 sections. In each section, glue an animal habitat picture.

4. Review the animals and habitats featured. Ask volunteers to tell what they know about these animals and where they live. Help students to do further research by looking through the encyclopedia and library books.

5. After students are more familiar with the animals and habitats, let them play a game with the wheel and clothespins. Mix up the clothespins and ask two students at a time to take turns attaching each clothespin to the habitat where that animal can be found. (Answers may vary.)

6. Store the wheel and clothespins in a folder with pockets and place on a shelf for use during free time.

© 1996 Troll Early Learning Activities

desert

underground

air

rain forest

Arctic

plains

forest

ocean

H abitat Wheel

© 1996 Troll Early Learning Activities

Habitat Wheel

© 1996 Troll Early Learning Activities

Life Cycle Sequence Cards

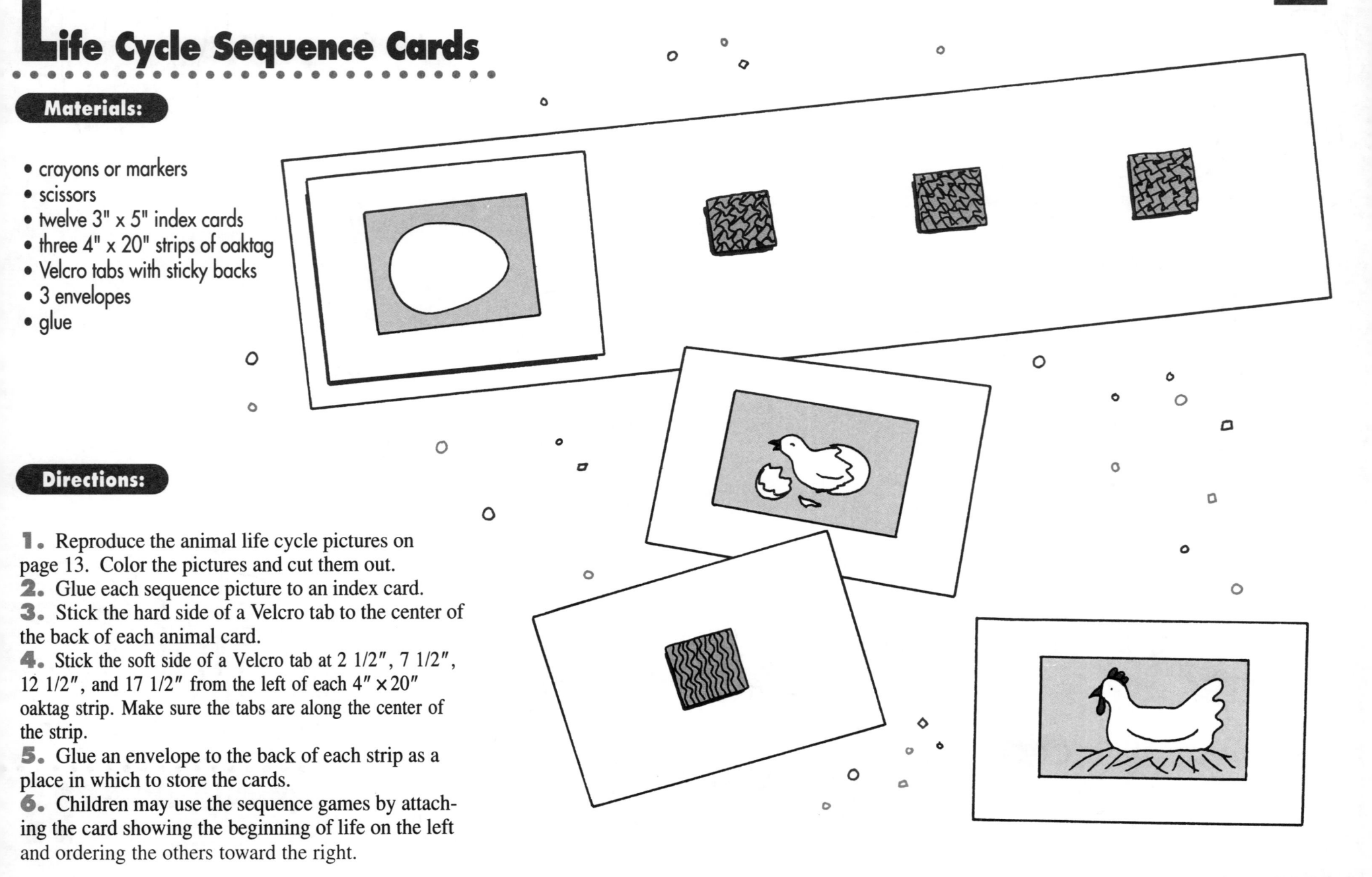

Materials:

- crayons or markers
- scissors
- twelve 3" x 5" index cards
- three 4" x 20" strips of oaktag
- Velcro tabs with sticky backs
- 3 envelopes
- glue

Directions:

1. Reproduce the animal life cycle pictures on page 13. Color the pictures and cut them out.

2. Glue each sequence picture to an index card.

3. Stick the hard side of a Velcro tab to the center of the back of each animal card.

4. Stick the soft side of a Velcro tab at 2 1/2″, 7 1/2″, 12 1/2″, and 17 1/2″ from the left of each 4″ × 20″ oaktag strip. Make sure the tabs are along the center of the strip.

5. Glue an envelope to the back of each strip as a place in which to store the cards.

6. Children may use the sequence games by attaching the card showing the beginning of life on the left and ordering the others toward the right.

© 1996 Troll Early Learning Activities

Life Cycle Sequence Cards

© 1996 Troll Early Learning Activities

Fill in the Categories

· · · · · · · · · · · · · · · · · · ·

Look at the animal pictures in the column on the left. Then fill in each box under the different categories with a word that begins with the same letter as the name of the animal in that row. The first row has been done for you.

Animals	Food	Clothing	Place
	melon	mittens	Mexico

© 1996 Troll Early Learning Activities

Animal Sounds Games

Oink, Oink Circle Game

1. Gather the class together in a circle. Choose a leader.

2. The leader begins the game by saying, "Oink!" The next player must say, "Oink, oink!" The third player repeats the sound three times, and so on around the circle.

3. Players who miscount or laugh are out of the game, and a new round begins. The new leader is the player whose turn is next.

4. Tell the new leader to choose another animal sound and begin the game again.

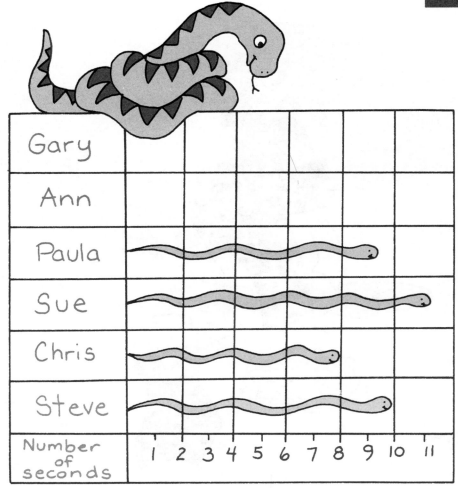

	1	2	3	4	5	6	7	8	9	10	11
Gary											
Ann											
Paula											
Sue											
Chris											
Steve											
Number of seconds	1	2	3	4	5	6	7	8	9	10	11

Hiss, Hiss Circle Game

1. Gather the class together in a circle. Choose one child to go first. Ask that student to make a continuous hissing sound for as long as possible. Time the player with the rest of the class. Then see who can hiss the longest.

2. Try the game with these sounds: buzz, meow, growl, and whistle.

3. On a large piece of oaktag or on the chalkboard, make a graph to show the amounts of time students can hiss, etc. After students become more familiar with the concept of graphing, let each child graph his or her results.

© 1996 Troll Early Learning Activities

Lily Pad Relay Race

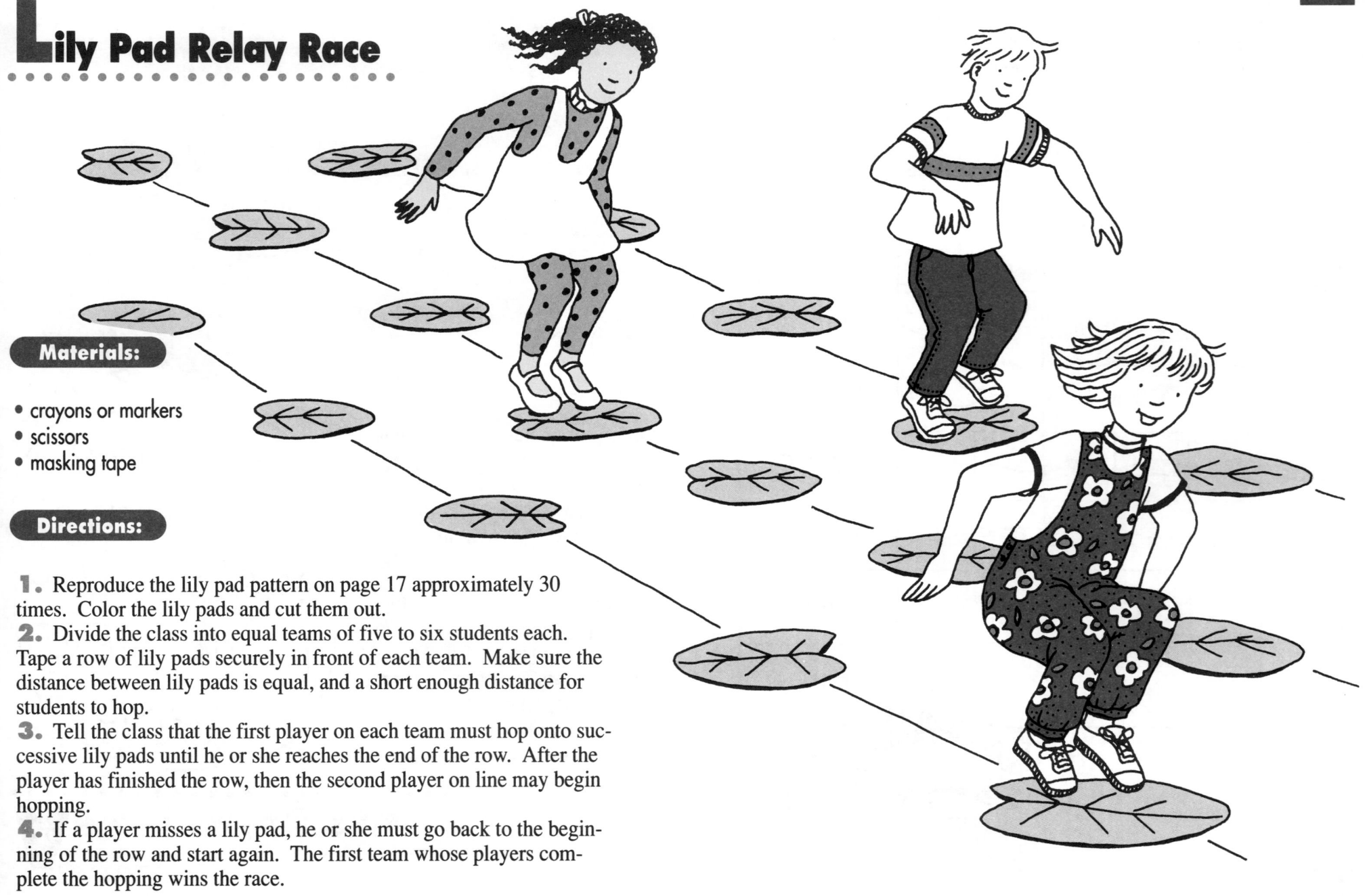

Materials:

• crayons or markers
• scissors
• masking tape

Directions:

1. Reproduce the lily pad pattern on page 17 approximately 30 times. Color the lily pads and cut them out.

2. Divide the class into equal teams of five to six students each. Tape a row of lily pads securely in front of each team. Make sure the distance between lily pads is equal, and a short enough distance for students to hop.

3. Tell the class that the first player on each team must hop onto successive lily pads until he or she reaches the end of the row. After the player has finished the row, then the second player on line may begin hopping.

4. If a player misses a lily pad, he or she must go back to the beginning of the row and start again. The first team whose players complete the hopping wins the race.

© 1996 Troll Early Learning Activities

Lily Pad Relay Race

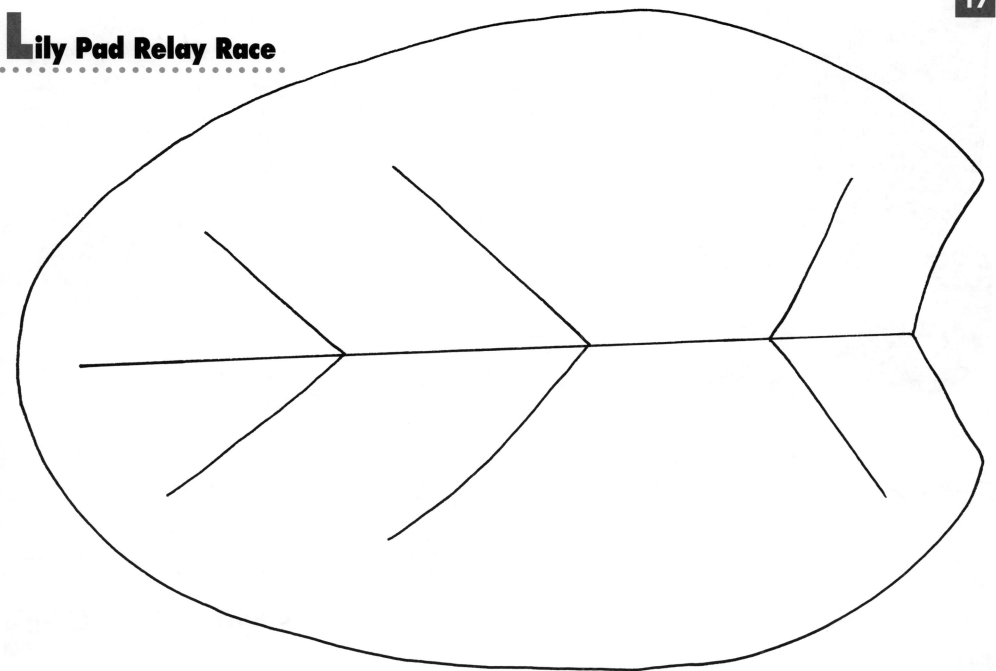

© 1996 Troll Early Learning Activities

Do This! Circle Game

1. Gather the class together in a circle. Students should remain standing.
2. Choose a leader. The leader must decide on an animal action and perform it for the player to his or her right. Actions may be anything, within reason, that an animal would do: scratch head, beat chest, hop, bark, blow bubbles, growl.
3. The player on the leader's right then performs the same action for the player on his or her right, and so on around the circle until it comes back to the leader. The player to the leader's right becomes the next leader.
4. After each round, discuss what types of animals might make each noise. Bring up discussion questions with the class, such as:

Why do animals make noises?
Do you think animals talk to each other?
What animals make the loudest noises?
Which ones make the softest noises?
What is your favorite animal sound?

Preposition Flip Cards

Materials:

- crayons or markers
- scissors
- 3" x 5" index cards
- glue
- clear contact paper
- clear tape
- permanent markers

Directions:

1. Reproduce the animal pictures on page 20. Color the pictures and cut them out.

2. Glue each picture to a 3" x 5" index card.

3. Make a flip cover for each index card by cutting 3" x 5" pieces of clear contact paper and sticking them together, sticky side in. Tape the cover to the card with clear tape along the top, as shown.

4. Using permanent markers, draw a picture on the contact paper emphasizing a preposition. For example, a picture of waves on the contact paper would make the whale picture seem as though it were swimming IN the ocean; or, drawing a banana NEXT to the gorilla.

5. Store the flip cards with the contact paper folded in the back. Children will look at the picture card first, then flip the contact paper cover over it and describe what they see.

Preposition Flip Cards

© 1994 Troll Early Learning Activities

Pin the Tail on the Stingray

Materials:

- crayons or markers
- scissors
- large sheet of oaktag
- glue
- tape
- blindfold

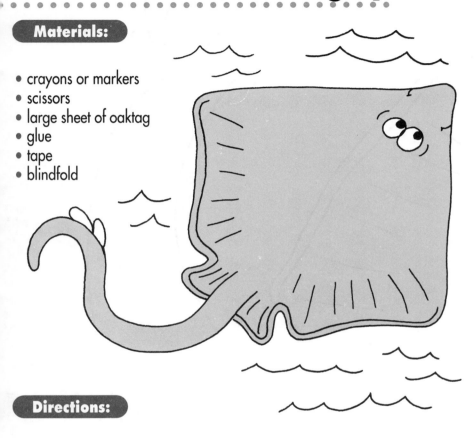

Directions:

1. Reproduce the stingray pattern on page 22 once and the tail once for each child in the class. Color the patterns and cut them out.

2. Glue the stingray body onto a large sheet of oaktag. Draw a sea picture around it.

3. Give each player a tail with a piece of tape at the top.

4. Place a blindfold on the first player and spin him or her around three times. Point the player in the direction of the stingray. The player must try to tape the tail onto the stingray in the proper position.

5. The player who comes closest to the correct tail position is the winner.

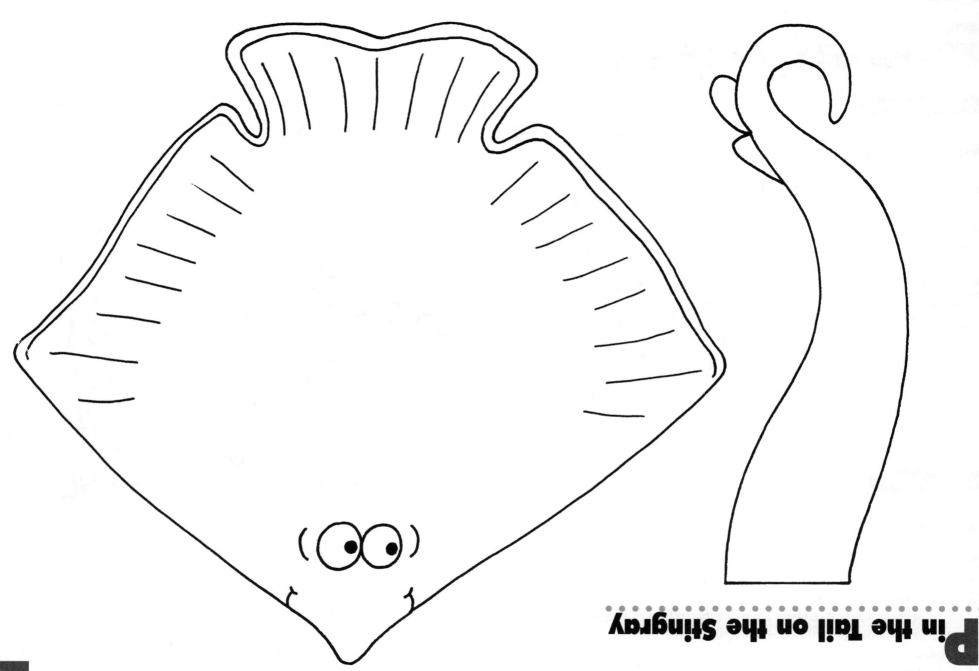

Pin the Tail on the Stingray

© 1996 Troll Early Learning Activities

Flour-and-Water Rattlesnake

Materials:

- package of long balloons
- package of small round balloons
- flour
- water
- mixing bowls
- newspaper strips
- safety pin
- scissors
- beans
- paints and paintbrushes

Directions:

1. Distribute one long balloon to each child. Blow up the balloons and knot the ends.

2. Mix one cup of flour with water in a mixing bowl. Gradually add the water while mixing until the mixture is thick but pourable.

3. Dip newspaper strips into the mixture and pull each strip through your thumb and fore-finger to get rid of any excess. Wrap the newspaper strips smoothly around the long balloon.

4. Cover the balloon with two layers of newspaper strips. After the strips have dried, stick a pin in the shape to pop the balloon.

5. Blow the round balloons up to about 3" in diameter. Then repeat the process by covering the round balloons with newspaper strips, then popping the balloons.

6. Cut a cross into the base of the round part and fit it onto one end of the long part. When the fit is tight, remove the round part, put about 20 beans into it, then fit it back on.

7. Using the flour and water mixture and newspaper strips once more, secure the round part to the long part by covering the spot where the two meet.

8. When dry, create a design on the rattler with paints. When the "tail" is shaken, the "snake" will rattle.

© 1996 Troll Early Learning Activities

What's My Name? Game

1. Gather the class together and choose one person to go out of the room. While that player is out, choose an animal name and an unrelated word.

2. Instruct the players that they may give clues to the person who left the room, but they must substitute the unrelated word each time they want to say the animal's name. For example, if the animal name is "sea turtle" and the unrelated word is "carpet," the exchange might go like this: "This carpet can swim. Carpets have hard shells, four legs, and a tail. These carpets lay their eggs on the beach."

3. Invite the excluded player back into the room. Tell him or her that the class thought up an animal name and he or she must guess it. Give the player three tries to guess the animal name. If the player guesses the name, he or she may pick the next player to go out of the room.

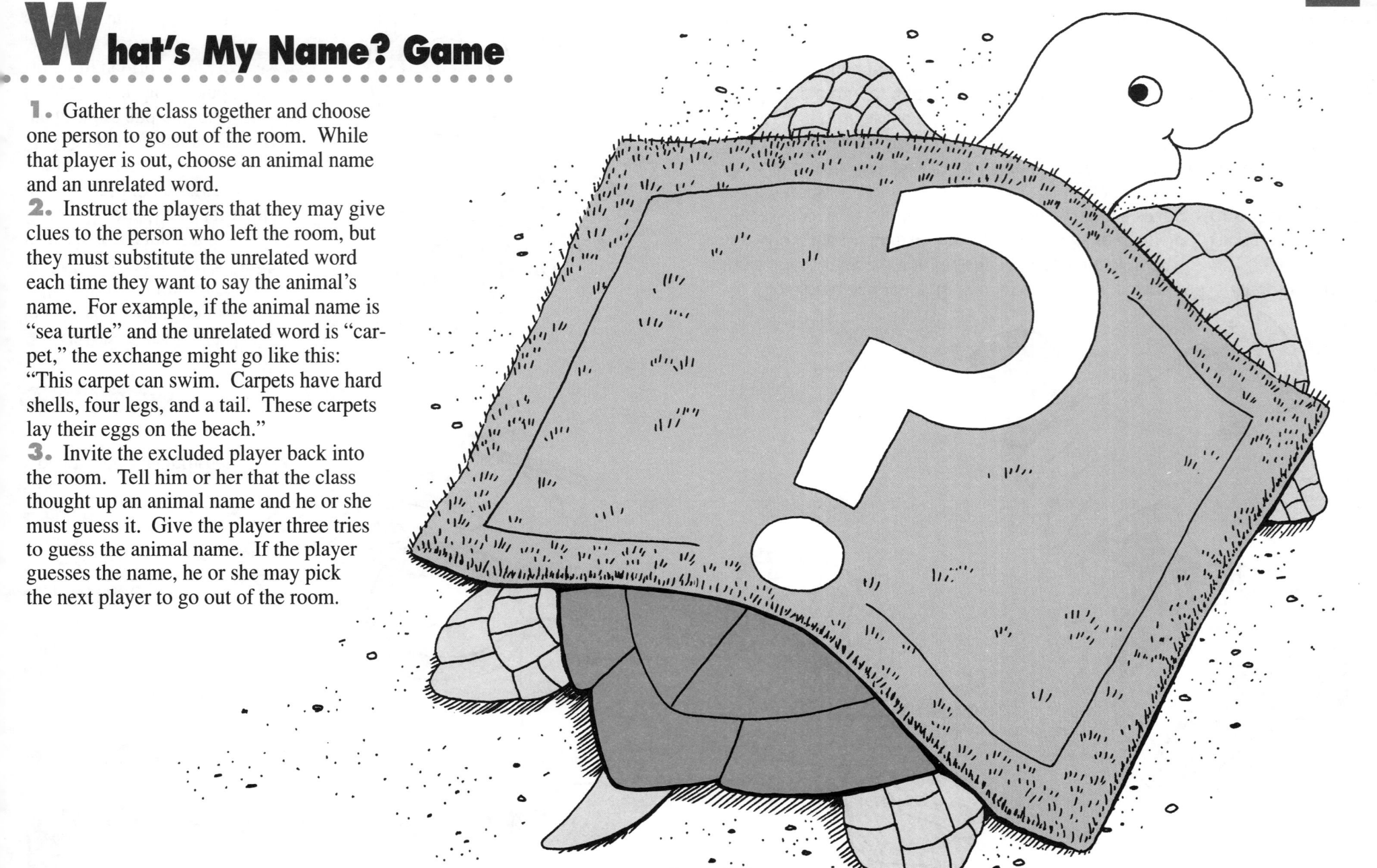

© 1996 Troll Early Learning Activities

Butterfly Cake Recipe

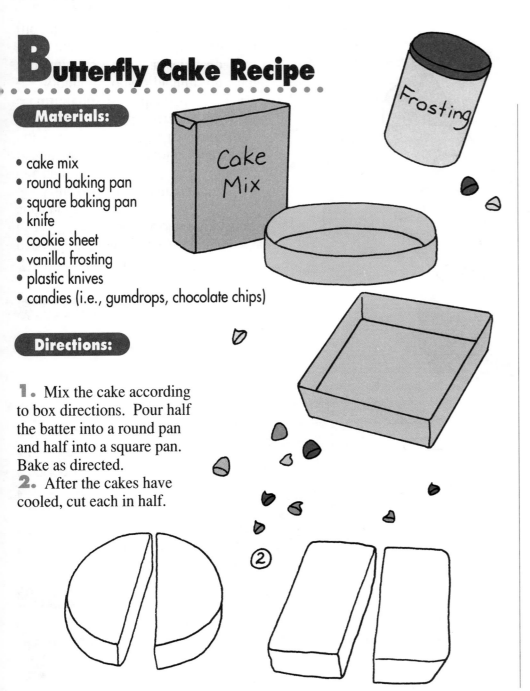

- cake mix
- round baking pan
- square baking pan
- knife
- cookie sheet
- vanilla frosting
- plastic knives
- candies (i.e., gumdrops, chocolate chips)

Directions:

1. Mix the cake according to box directions. Pour half the batter into a round pan and half into a square pan. Bake as directed.
2. After the cakes have cooled, cut each in half.

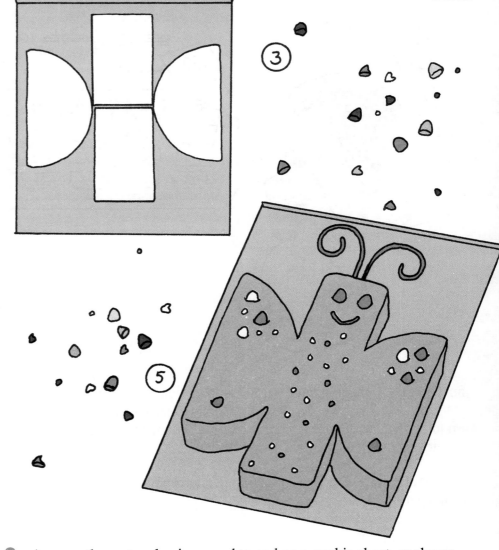

3. Arrange the rectangle pieces end to end on a cookie sheet, as shown. This is the butterfly body. Then place a half circle in the middle of each side of the body.
4. Give students plastic knives to use to frost the butterfly.
5. Decorate the butterfly using candies. Make eyes, antennae, and patterns on the wings and body.

Animals Helping People Lotto Game

Materials:

- crayons or markers
- scissors
- letter-sized file folder
- glue
- oaktag
- clear contact paper
- envelope

How to Play the Game:

1. Shuffle the playing cards and place them face down in a pile to one side of the open file folder.

2. The youngest player goes first. That player takes a card from the top of the pile and matches it to the animal that provides the service or product featured.

3. Play continues as the next player takes a card and matches it to an animal on his or her game board. If a player takes a card he or she cannot use, the card is placed in a discard pile.

4. The first player to match all of his or her animal pictures with playing cards is the winner.

Directions:

1. Reproduce the animal pictures on page 27 twice and the object pictures on page 28 three times. Color the pictures and cut them out.

2. Glue one set of animal pictures on one half of the inside of a file folder, facing away from the fold. Glue the other set to the other half, also facing away from the fold. Arrange the second set differently from the first.

3. Mount the object pictures on oaktag and laminate with clear contact paper.

4. Glue an envelope on the back of the file folder to store the playing cards.

© 1996 Troll Early Learning Activities

Animals Helping People Lotto Game

© 1996 Troll Early Learning Activities

Animals Helping People Lotto Game

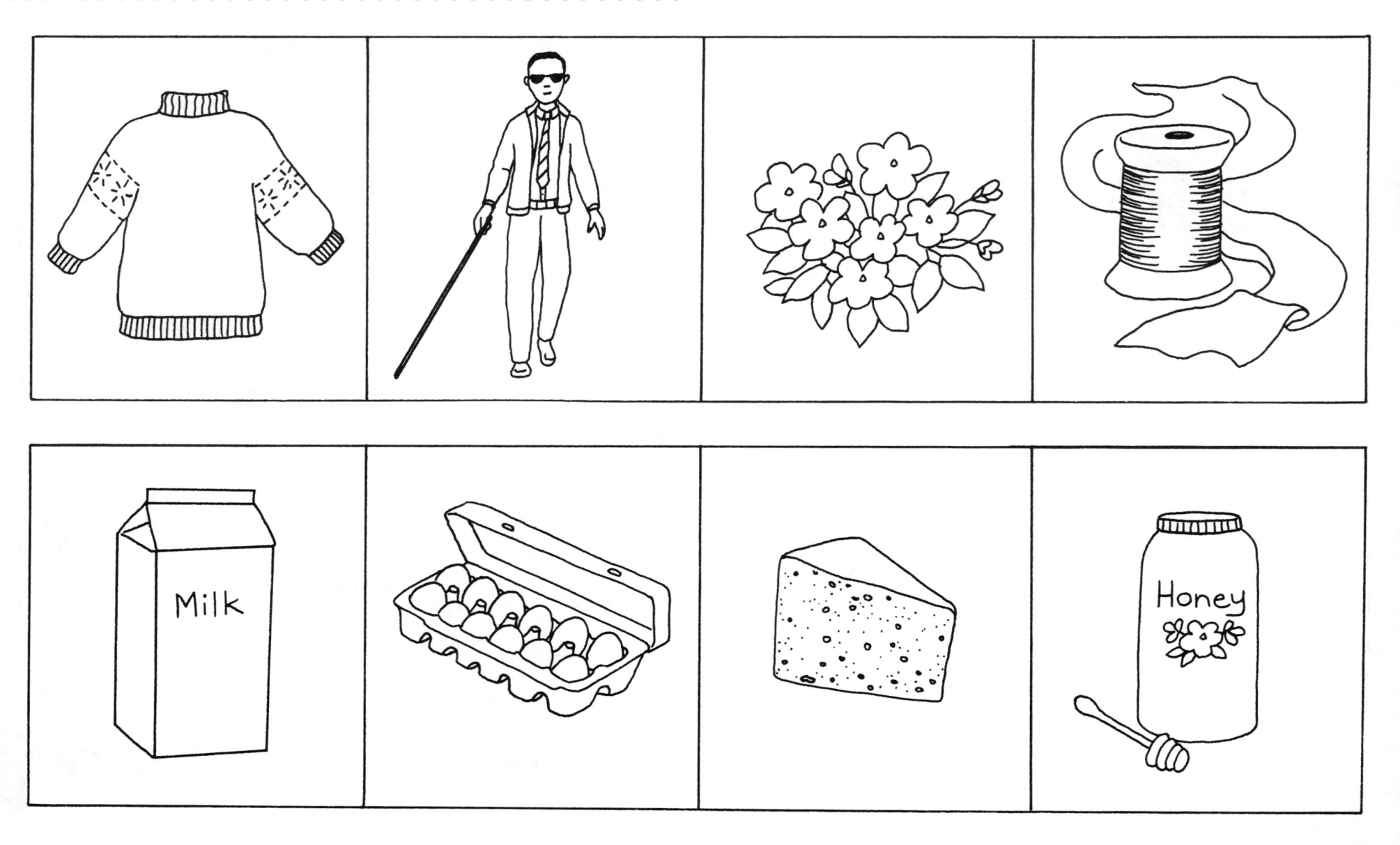

© 1996 Troll Early Learning Activities

Mother and Baby Game

MOTHER and BABY GAME

Materials:

- crayons or markers
- scissors
- oaktag
- glue
- egg carton

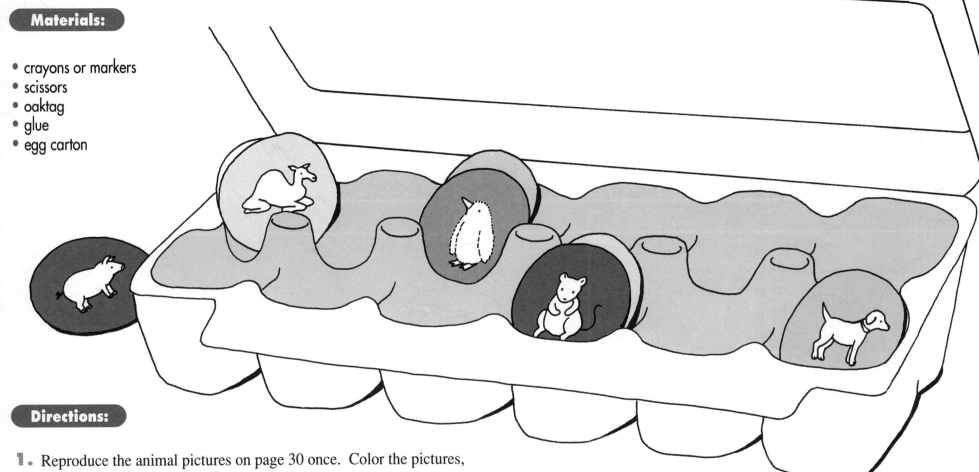

Directions:

1. Reproduce the animal pictures on page 30 once. Color the pictures, mount them on oaktag, and cut them out.

2. Decorate the outside of the egg carton so children will know what game is inside.

3. Gently push a mother animal picture into each egg carton depression so they face up and stay in place.

4. To play, tell students to match the baby animal card to the mother animal by placing the baby's picture in front of the mother's.

© 1996 Troll Early Learning Activities

Mother and Baby Game

© 1996 Troll Early Learning Activities

Which One Doesn't Belong? Banner

Materials:

- crayons or markers
- scissors
- small index cards
- glue
- wire hanger
- large sheet of oaktag (as wide as the hanger)
- stapler
- clear contact paper
- transparent tape

Directions:

1. Reproduce some animal pictures from this unit once. Color the pictures and cut them out.

2. Glue each animal picture onto an index card.

3. Fold the top 1" of a large piece of oaktag over the base of a wire hanger and staple it in place so it hangs from the hanger, as shown.

4. With clear contact paper, make four pockets for the banner. Cut two 5" x 7" squares and place them together, sticky side in. Then tape the pockets to the middle of the banner using clear tape.

5. Place one animal picture in each pocket. Make one animal different from the others. (For example, three of the animals might have four feet, the last one only two.)

6. To play, ask students to discover which animal does not belong with the others and tell why. Continue with the other animal groupings. When the children have become more familiar with the game, allow them to create new animal groupings.

© 1996 Troll Early Learning Activities

Endangered Animals Magnets

Materials:

- crayons or markers
- scissors
- corrugated cardboard scraps
- glue
- magnet strips, with sticky backs

Directions:

1. Reproduce the endangered animals pictures on page 33. Color the pictures and cut them out.

2. Glue the pictures onto corrugated cardboard. Cut the excess cardboard away.

3. Stick a magnet strip to the back of the cardboard. Attach the magnets to the chalkboard for all to view the different endangered animals.

4. Ask children to explain what they think the word "endangered" means. Write all the comments on experience chart paper. Inform the class that an animal that is endangered is in danger of extinction in all or a large amount of its ranges. When an animal is extinct, there can never be another one again; the whole species has died out.

5. Ask children to think of why some animals today may become extinct. Explain that some animals are in danger because of humans. Population growth, expansion into animal habitats, pollution, and excessive hunting are some of the human activities responsible for endangering animals.

6. Help students make a class book about being endangered from an animal's perspective. Encourage the children to write and illustrate a story featuring the chosen animal.

7. Children may wish to create a cover using the pictures from page 33. Place the finished book on the bookshelf for reading during library or free time.

The Bald Eagle: An Endangered Animal

© 1996 Troll Early Learning Activities

Endangered Animals Magnets

© 1996 Troll Early Learning Activities

Dinosaur Masks

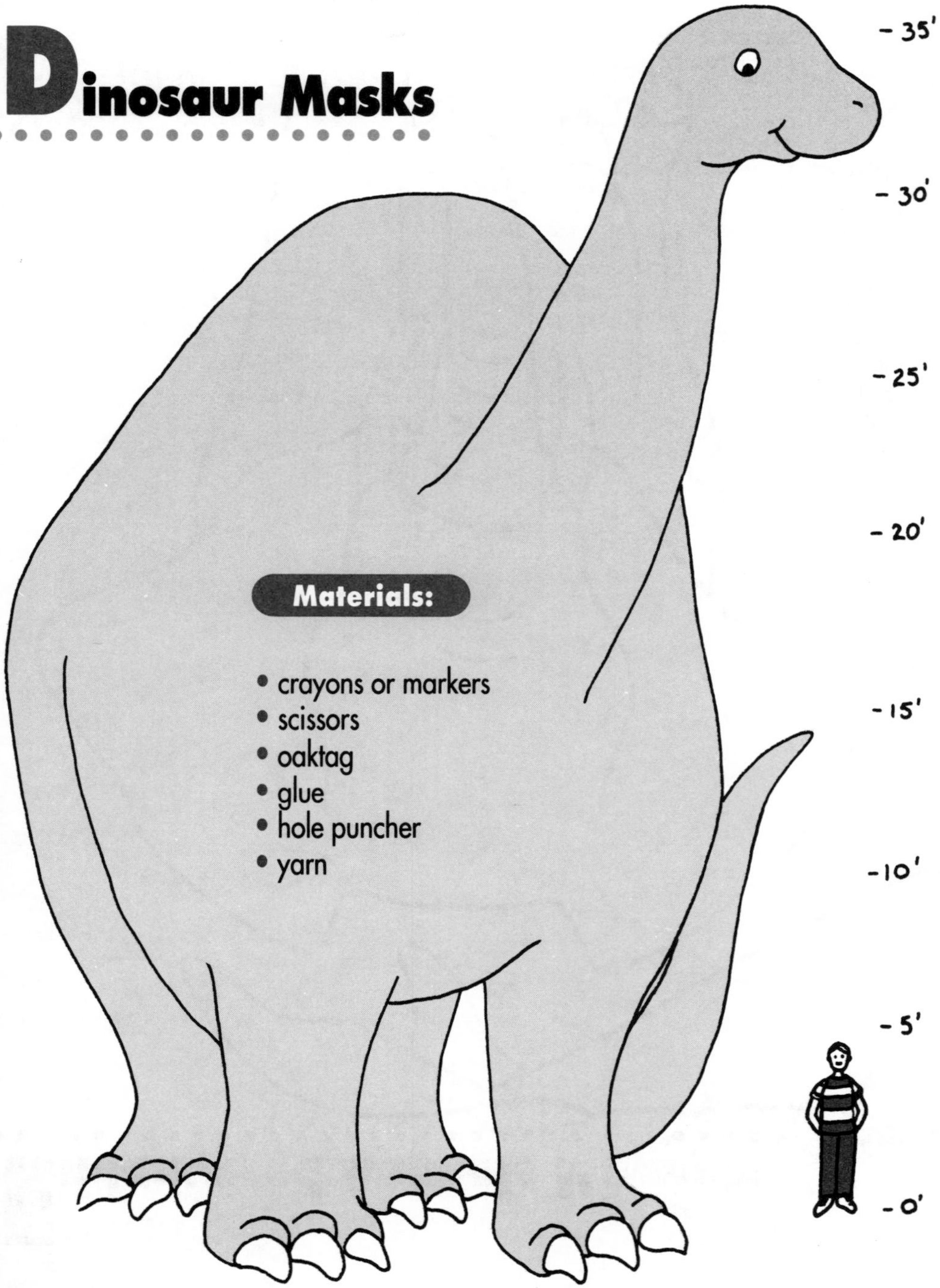

– 35'

– 30'

– 25'

– 20'

© 1996 Troll Early Learning Activities

Materials:

- crayons or markers
- scissors
- oaktag
- glue
- hole puncher
- yarn

– 15'

– 10'

– 5'

– 0'

Directions:

1. Ask each child to select one of the dinosaur face patterns on pages 35 and 36 to use to make a mask. Reproduce the selected mask once for each child.

2. Have each student color the face and cut it out. Then help each child glue the face onto oaktag. Trim away any excess.

3. Punch holes on both sides of the dinosaur face.

4. Tie a 10" length of yarn to each hole, as shown. Tie the mask to fit around each child's head.

5. Display books about dinosaurs in the classroom. If possible, arrange for a class field trip to see exhibits about dinosaurs in nearby museums. Help students imagine the size of a dinosaur by comparing it to something at school or home. Inform the class of dinosaur names—children love to try to pronounce the complicated names!

6. Ask children if there are any live dinosaurs around today. Discuss the term "extinction" with the class. Try to theorize with the children why the dinosaurs might have died out (glacial expansion, food supply disappeared, temperature changes).

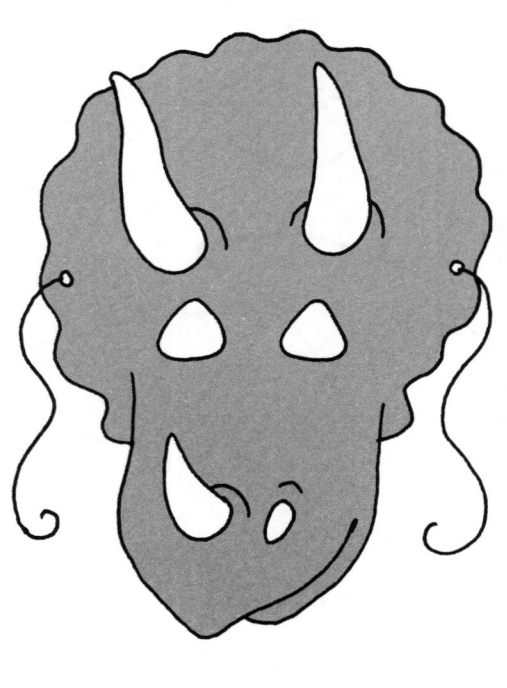

Dinosaur Masks

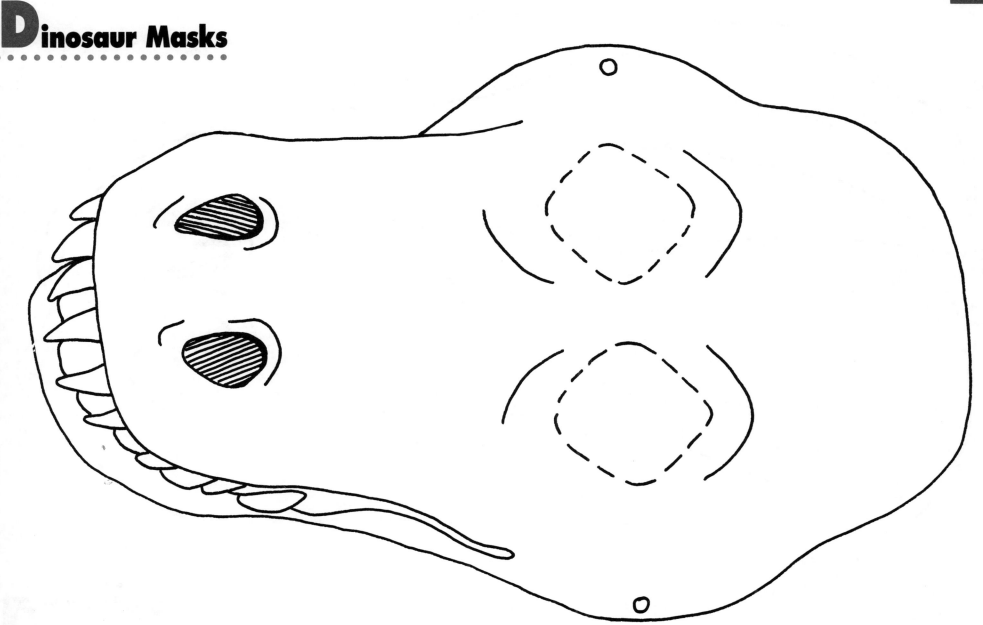

© 1996 Troll Early Learning Activities

© 1996 Troll Early Learning Activities

Dinosaur Masks

Animal Groups Bulletin Board

1. Have a class discussion about the different groups of animals that exist. Try to keep the categories fairly simple, such as:

    Mammals
    Reptiles and Amphibians
    Fish
    Birds
    Insects

2. Explain that there are general physiological differences between these groups. For example, mammals are warm-blooded, give birth to live young, and have some hair or fur. Reptiles are cold-blooded, usually lay eggs, and have dry, sometimes scaly skin. Amphibians may have lungs and/or gills for breathing in air underwater, lay eggs, and live on land and in the water. Fish are cold-blooded and live in water. Birds are warm-blooded, are covered with feathers, usually fly, and lay eggs. Insects are the largest group of animals. They have three body divisions and six legs, but they do not have lungs. (Spiders are in their own group, called Arachnids.)

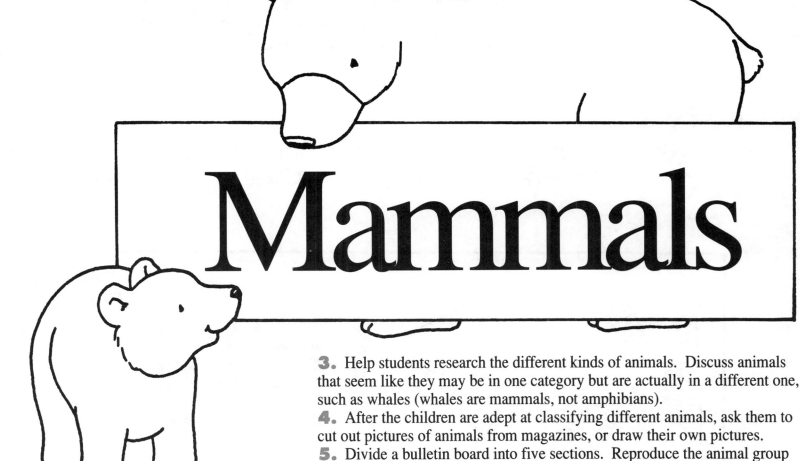

3. Help students research the different kinds of animals. Discuss animals that seem like they may be in one category but are actually in a different one, such as whales (whales are mammals, not amphibians).

4. After the children are adept at classifying different animals, ask them to cut out pictures of animals from magazines, or draw their own pictures.

5. Divide a bulletin board into five sections. Reproduce the animal group signs on this page and pages 38 and 39 once. Attach one sign to the top of each section.

6. Let students attach their pictures collage-style in the appropriate sections. You may also wish to write key words about each group on index cards and attach them to the board under each group. Title the bulletin board "Wonderful World of Animals."

© 1996 Troll Early Learning Activities

© 1996 Troll Early Learning Activities

Insects

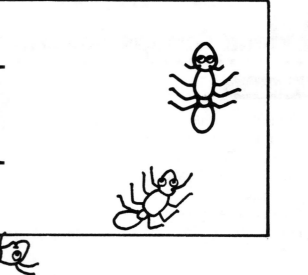

Fish

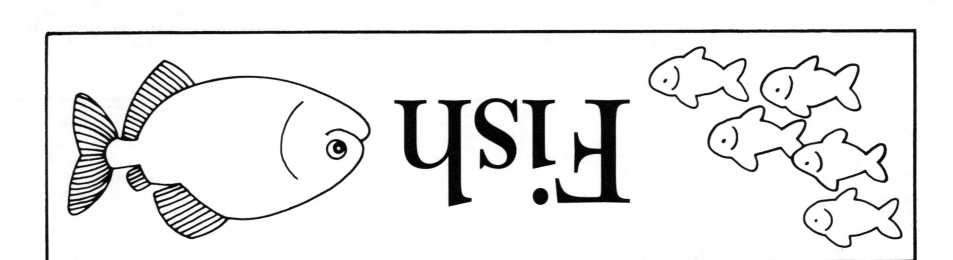

Animal Groups Bulletin Board

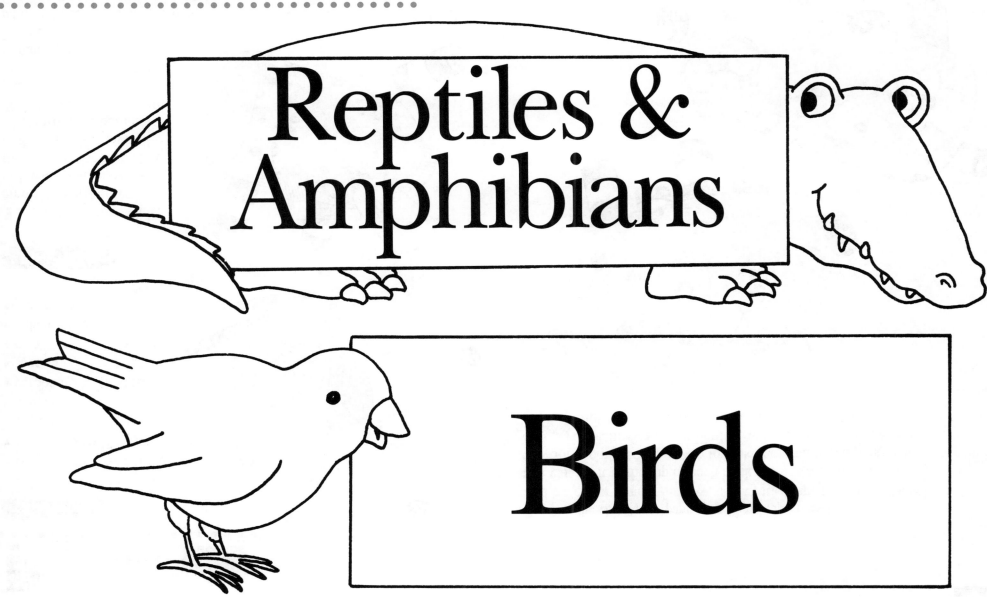

Reptiles & Amphibians

Birds

© 1996 Troll Early Learning Activities

Piggy Bank Math

Materials:

- clean, empty plastic bottles
- paints and paintbrushes or permanent markers
- liquid detergent
- cardboard toilet paper rolls
- scissors
- glue
- buttons or sequins
- pipe cleaners

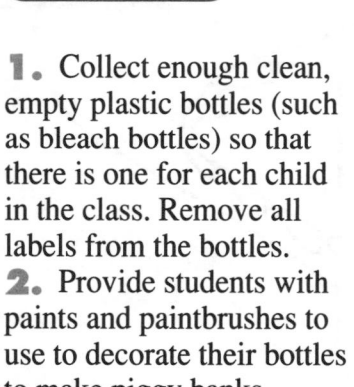

Directions:

1. Collect enough clean, empty plastic bottles (such as bleach bottles) so that there is one for each child in the class. Remove all labels from the bottles.

2. Provide students with paints and paintbrushes to use to decorate their bottles to make piggy banks. Before using, mix each paint with some liquid detergent to help the paint stick to the plastic bottle. Or, give students permanent markers to use to decorate their piggy banks.

3. Help students use cardboard toilet paper rolls to make legs for their piggy banks. Cut the rolls to about 3" in length. Then glue the rolls to the bottom of each bottle, as shown, and paint.

4. Tell the children to paint each bottle cap to resemble a pig's snout. Add buttons or sequins for eyes, and a curled pipe cleaner for the tail.

5. Cut a slit in the top of each bank for students to insert money.

6. Some children may wish to make nontraditional piggy banks by painting designs or pictures on their bottles, and adding collage materials, such as sequins, pipe cleaners, buttons, and yarn.

Cause and Effect

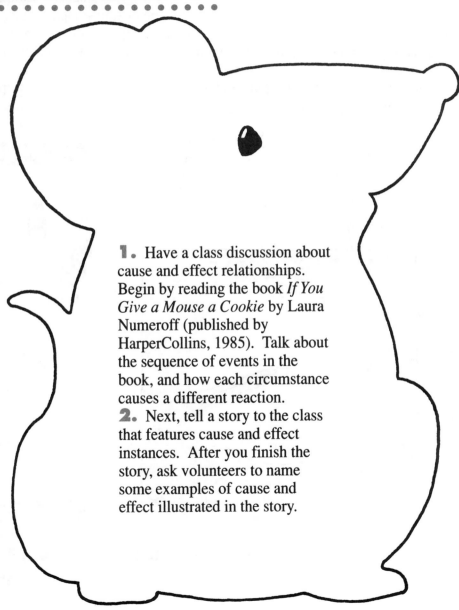

1. Have a class discussion about cause and effect relationships. Begin by reading the book *If You Give a Mouse a Cookie* by Laura Numeroff (published by HarperCollins, 1985). Talk about the sequence of events in the book, and how each circumstance causes a different reaction.

2. Next, tell a story to the class that features cause and effect instances. After you finish the story, ask volunteers to name some examples of cause and effect illustrated in the story.

3. Reproduce the mouse outline on this page once and cut it out. Trace the mouse onto white paper twenty times.

4. Write some of the cause and effect relationships described by students from the book you read. Sum up the causes on one mouse, and the effects on another mouse. Place the mouse pairs next to each other on the chalkboard or bulletin board.

5. Ask students to think about cause and effect instances that happen in everyday life. Give them some examples to get them started, such as:

If I don't clean my room,...   If I do my homework,...

If I'm mean to my little brother,...   If I don't waste water,...

Have volunteers tell what might happen in these instances. Write down students' comments on new pairs of cause and effect mice.

Hickory Dickory Dock

Materials:

- crayons or markers
- glue
- oaktag
- scissors
- pencils
- brass fasteners
- large toy clock

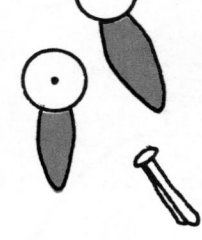

Directions:

1. Reproduce the grandfather clock and hands on page 43 once for each child. Have students color the clocks and hands, mount them on oaktag, and cut them out.

2. Help each student use a pencil to poke a hole through the end of each hand and the center of the clock face, as shown.

3. Show students how to attach the hands to the center of their clock faces with brass fasteners.

4. Using a large toy clock, demonstrate the different hours of the day, beginning with 7 o'clock (waking up). Ask the children to move the hands of their clocks along with you as you progress through a typical student day.

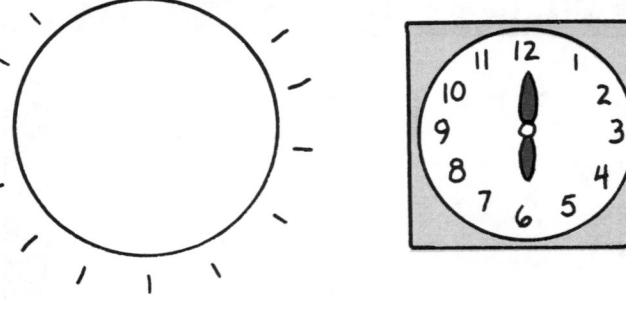

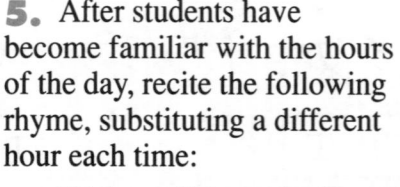

5. After students have become familiar with the hours of the day, recite the following rhyme, substituting a different hour each time:

> Hickory dickory dock,
> Now it's _____ o'clock.

Ask students to move the hands of their clocks to correspond to the specific hour from the rhyme.

6. Once the children understand the hours of the day, use the clocks to introduce the concept of half hours and quarter hours.

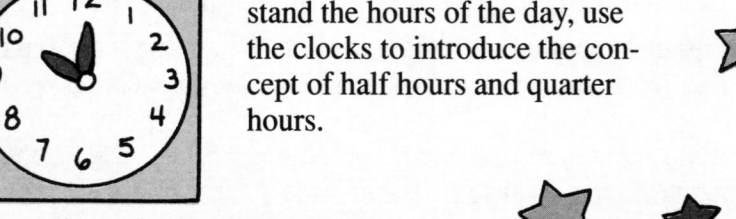

© 1996 Troll Early Learning Activities

Hickory Dickory Dock

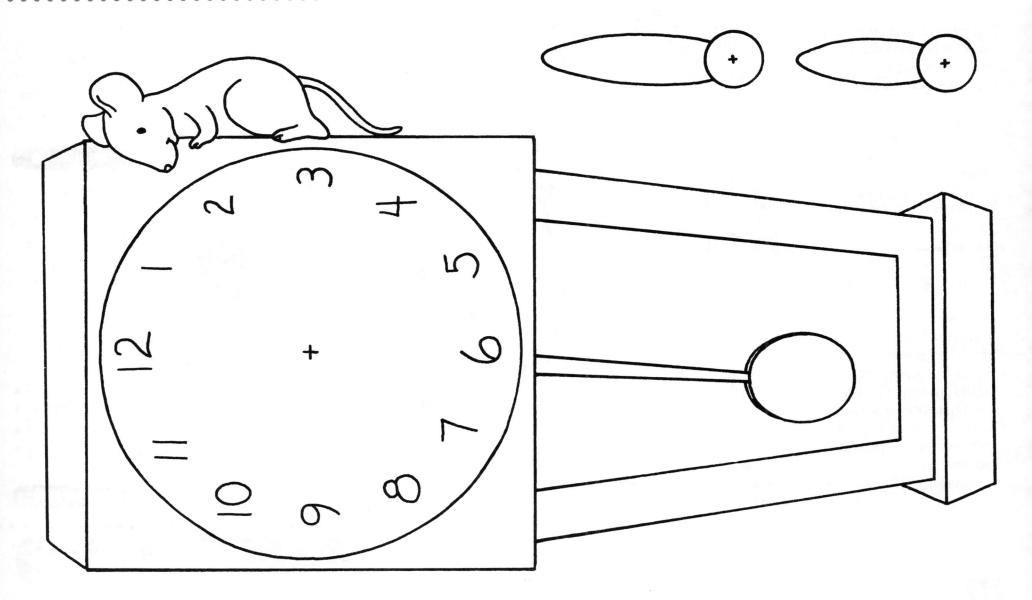

© 1996 Troll Early Learning Activities

Curious George Big Book

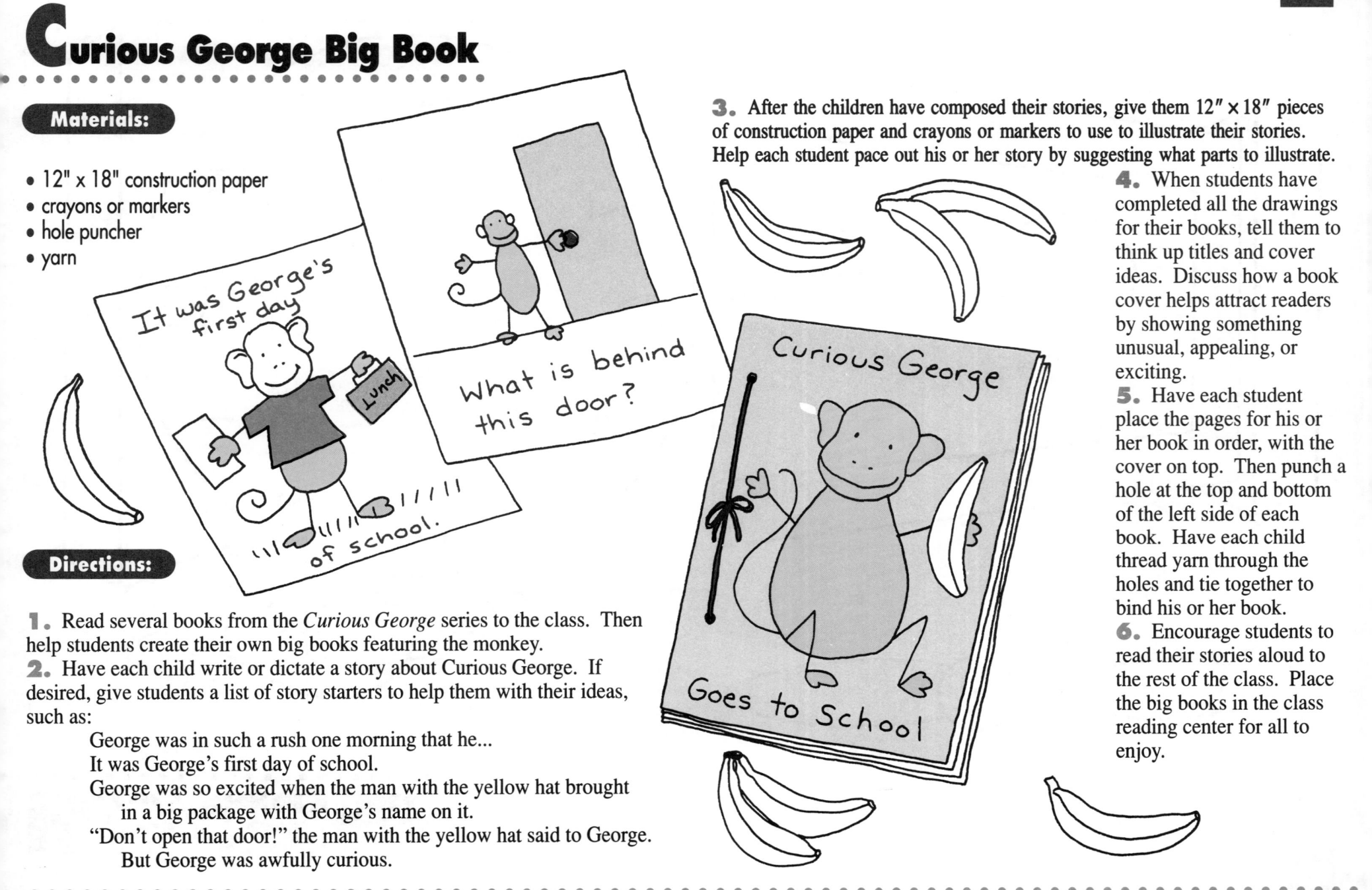

Materials:

- 12" x 18" construction paper
- crayons or markers
- hole puncher
- yarn

It was George's first day

Lunch

of school.

What is behind this door?

Curious George

Goes to School

Directions:

1. Read several books from the *Curious George* series to the class. Then help students create their own big books featuring the monkey.

2. Have each child write or dictate a story about Curious George. If desired, give students a list of story starters to help them with their ideas, such as:

George was in such a rush one morning that he...
It was George's first day of school.
George was so excited when the man with the yellow hat brought in a big package with George's name on it.
"Don't open that door!" the man with the yellow hat said to George. But George was awfully curious.

3. After the children have composed their stories, give them 12" x 18" pieces of construction paper and crayons or markers to use to illustrate their stories. Help each student pace out his or her story by suggesting what parts to illustrate.

4. When students have completed all the drawings for their books, tell them to think up titles and cover ideas. Discuss how a book cover helps attract readers by showing something unusual, appealing, or exciting.

5. Have each student place the pages for his or her book in order, with the cover on top. Then punch a hole at the top and bottom of the left side of each book. Have each child thread yarn through the holes and tie together to bind his or her book.

6. Encourage students to read their stories aloud to the rest of the class. Place the big books in the class reading center for all to enjoy.

© 1996 Troll Early Learning Activities

Truly Curious

Read the sentences below about Curious George. On the lines provided, write a "T" if the statement is true, and an "F" if it is false.

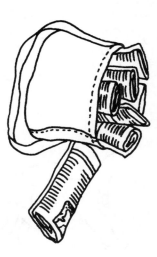

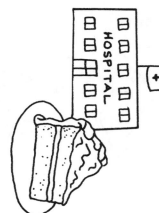

____ 1. The man with the yellow hat found George in Canada.

____ 2. George liked delivering newspapers on his bike.

____ 3. George had to go to the hospital because he ate a piece of cake.

____ 4. One day George accidentally called the fire station.

____ 5. George got a medal for traveling into space.

____ 6. George once starred in a movie.

____ 7. George's favorite fruit is apples.

____ 8. George is a very big monkey with blue fur.

____ 9. One day George made ducks out of newspapers and floated them in the water.

____ 10. George likes to find out about new things.

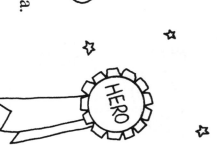

© 1996 Troll Early Learning Activities

Name _____

Monkey Match

Look at the silly monkeys on the left side of this page. Then circle each monkey's match in the row.

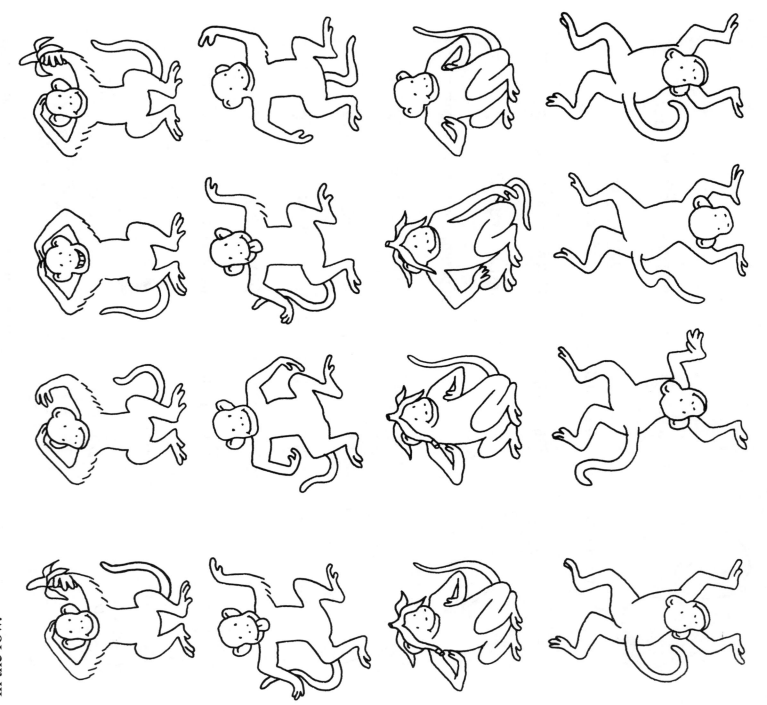

© 1996 Troll Early Learning Activities

Find the names of the 20 animals hidden in the puzzle below. The words may be hidden forward, backward, up, down, or diagonally.

Critter Search

```
D A O T S M A H A M S T E R
A T N A H P E L E N Q U A L
K O B B T G I R A F F E N Q
C A N A I M T I B A R T E Q
U N D L H A Q U E L G A E R
H S N L G I R E B Q A C C L
C R H I N O C E R O S R C A
D T P G L E R R I U Q S O H
O A O A T A L I N H I Q O W
O D L T I G D O L P H I N W
W E P O L E T N A L I U Q L
D O H R H I N C E K A N S R
```

dog	cat	antelope	tiger	gorilla
giraffe	rhinoceros	alligator	eagle	whale
toad	dolphin	snake	hamster	woodchuck
squirrel	elephant	rabbit	bear	raccoon

© 1996 Troll Early Learning Activities

The Bremen Town Musicians Flannel Board

A long, long time ago there lived an old donkey. One day the donkey's master told him that he must leave the farm because he was too old to work. The donkey decided to travel to Bremen and become a town musician.

After the donkey had traveled a short way, he saw a tired, old dog lying on the side of the road.

"Are you all right?" the donkey asked.

"No," said the dog sadly. "My master just told me that I must leave because I am too old to hunt for him. Oh, what will I do?"

"Come with me," said the donkey. "I am on my way to Bremen to become a town musician." And so the two new friends set off together.

After a while they met a forlorn little cat.

"Are you all right?" the donkey asked kindly.

"No," said the cat. "My master has put me out because I am too old and slow to catch mice for him. Oh, what will I do?"

"Come with us," said the donkey. "We are on our way to Bremen to become the town musicians." And so it happened that the cat joined the donkey and the dog.

Several hours later, the three came upon a rooster who was crowing painfully loudly.

"What is wrong?" brayed the donkey.

"Oh, I fear that I am not long for this world," crowed the rooster. "My master plans to cook me for Sunday supper."

"Then you must come with us," said the donkey. "We are on our way to Bremen to become the town musicians. Your crowing will be a happy addition to our group."

So the four new friends continued on their way to Bremen. Before too long, they decided to settle down for the night. They came upon a house nestled in the woods.

"This looks like a fine place for us," said the donkey. But when he looked in the window, he saw a band of robbers sitting down to a huge feast.

The donkey thought for a minute. Then he whispered an idea to his friends. The four animals began making as much noise as they could. When the robbers got up from the table to see what was making such a racket, the animals stormed through the front door.

The robbers were so surprised and frightened, they ran off into the woods without looking back. The animals sat down happily at the table and feasted for hours before they laid down for a good night's sleep.

Now, the robbers wanted to know what it was that had scared them away. They sent one man to the house to see. When he opened the door to the dark house, the cat jumped on the man and scratched him. The man ran to the back door, but he tripped over the dog. The dog bit the man in the shin. The man screamed and ran out through the courtyard, where the donkey kicked him as hard as he could. And all through the commotion the rooster crowed with all his might.

The terrified robber ran back to his band. "I can't believe I made it out of there alive!" he gasped. "First, a witch scratched me with her long fingernails. Then a man with a knife stabbed me in the shin. Next, a giant beat me with a big stick. And all through it a judge sitting on the roof cried out, "Bring him here!""

The robbers agreed to never go to the house again. And as for the Bremen town musicians, they decided the little house was the perfect place for them to live forever and ever. And so they did!

The Bremen Town Musicians Flannel Board

Reproduce the figures on this page and page 50 once. Color the figures and cut them out. Then place scraps of flannel or sandpaper on the back of each figure. Move the figures around a flannel board as you read "The Bremen Town Musicians."

© 1996 Troll Early Learning Activities

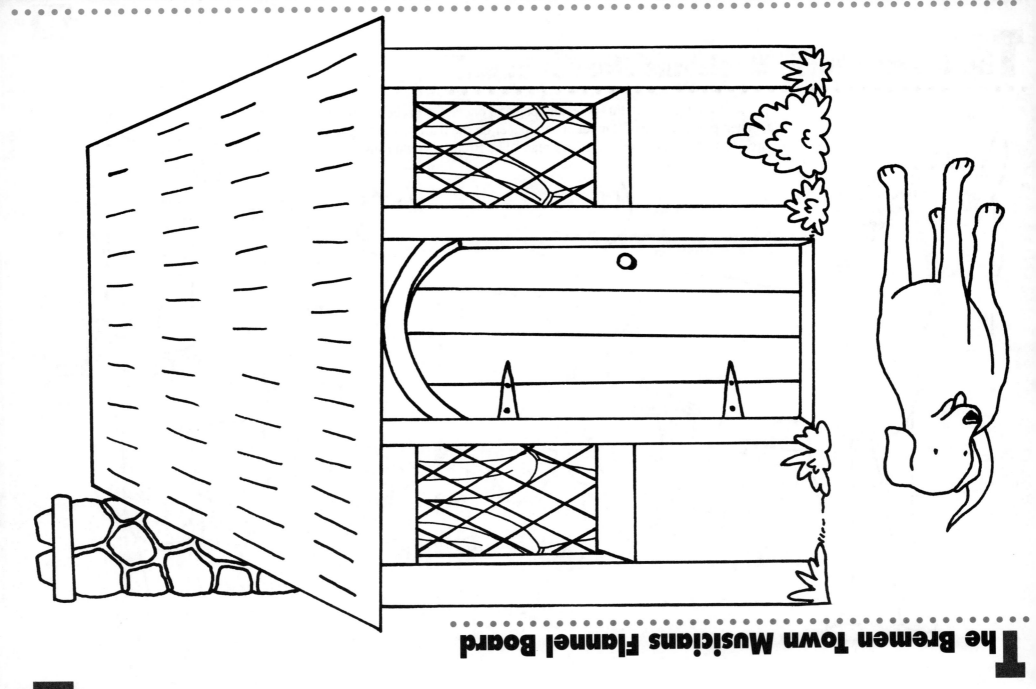

The Bremen Town Musicians Flannel Board

Which Animal Am I?

· · · · · · · · · · · · · ·

Draw a line to connect each animal with its description.

1. rabbit

2. whale

3. porcupine

4. wolf

5. armadillo

6. bat

7. frog

8. snake

9. zebra

10. cheetah

A. I'm a mammal that flies.

B. I live in lakes and ponds.

C. I live in a burrow.

D. I slither along the ground.

E. I'm the largest mammal.

F. I'm related to horses.

G. My quills protect me from enemies.

H. I'm the fastest mammal.

I. I hunt in packs.

J. I have skin like armor.

© 1996 Troll Early Learning Activities

Old Lady Finger Puppets

Materials:

- crayons or markers
- glue
- oaktag
- scissors
- stapler

Directions:

1. Reproduce the figures on pages 53 and 54 once. Color the figures, mount them on oaktag, and cut them out.

2. Attach a 1" x 3" oaktag strip to the back of each figure. Staple the strip together to fit around a finger, as shown.

3. Hold the finger puppets up while singing the song.

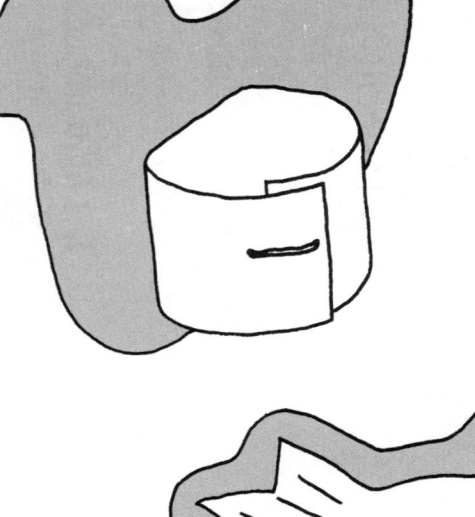

There was an old lady who swallowed a fly.
I don't know why she swallowed a fly.
Perhaps she'll die.

There was an old lady who swallowed a spider.
It wriggled and jiggled and squiggled inside her.
She swallowed the spider to catch the fly.
I don't know why she swallowed a fly.
Perhaps she'll die.

There was an old lady who swallowed a bird.
Oh, my word! She swallowed a bird.
She swallowed the bird to catch the spider.
She swallowed the spider to catch the fly....

There was an old lady who swallowed a cat.
Imagine that! She swallowed a cat.
She swallowed the cat to catch the bird....

There was an old lady who swallowed a dog.
What a hog! She swallowed a dog.
She swallowed the dog to catch the cat....

There was an old lady who swallowed a goat.
Right down her throat—she swallowed a goat.
She swallowed the goat to catch the dog....

There was an old lady who swallowed a cow.
I don't know how she swallowed a cow.
She swallowed the cow to catch the goat....

There was an old lady who swallowed a horse.
She died, of course!

© 1996 Troll Early Learning Activities

Old Lady Finger Puppets

© 1996 Troll Early Learning Activities

© 1994 Troll Early Learning Activities

Old Lady Finger Puppets

Animal Habitats Class Mural

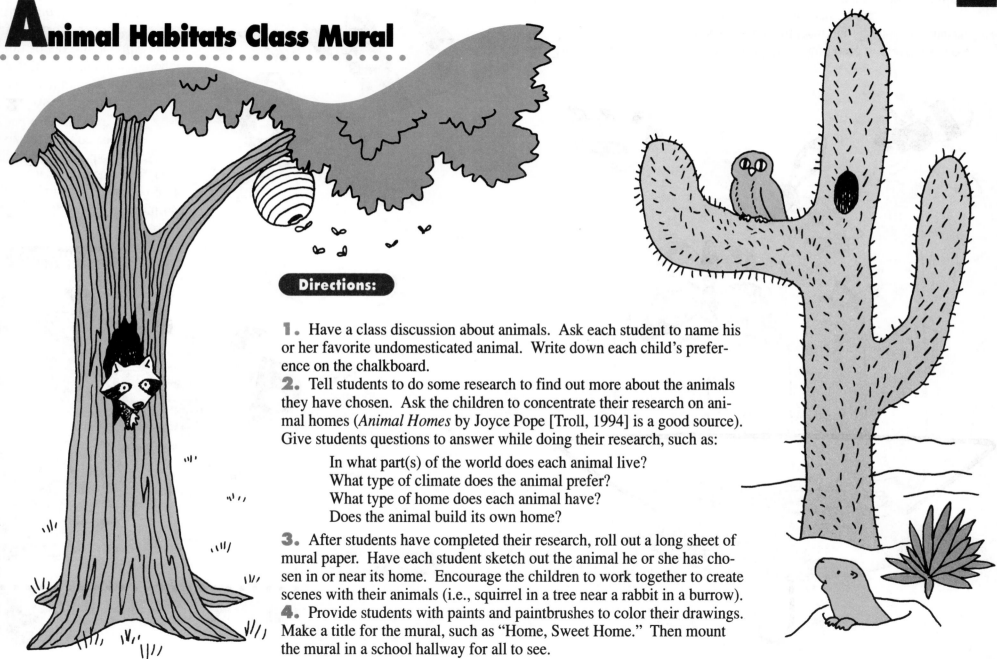

Directions:

1. Have a class discussion about animals. Ask each student to name his or her favorite undomesticated animal. Write down each child's preference on the chalkboard.

2. Tell students to do some research to find out more about the animals they have chosen. Ask the children to concentrate their research on animal homes (*Animal Homes* by Joyce Pope [Troll, 1994] is a good source). Give students questions to answer while doing their research, such as:

> In what part(s) of the world does each animal live?
> What type of climate does the animal prefer?
> What type of home does each animal have?
> Does the animal build its own home?

3. After students have completed their research, roll out a long sheet of mural paper. Have each student sketch out the animal he or she has chosen in or near its home. Encourage the children to work together to create scenes with their animals (i.e., squirrel in a tree near a rabbit in a burrow).

4. Provide students with paints and paintbrushes to color their drawings. Make a title for the mural, such as "Home, Sweet Home." Then mount the mural in a school hallway for all to see.

Flying Friends Mobile

Materials:

- crayons or markers
- glue
- oaktag
- scissors
- hole puncher
- yarn
- hangers
- tape

Directions:

1. Reproduce the figures and banner on pages 57 and 58 once for each child. Have students color the figures, mount them on oaktag, and cut them out.

2. Ask each child to punch a hole at the top of each animal. Then have students thread varying lengths of yarn (from 6" to 12") through the holes and tie, as shown.

3. Tie the figures to the bottom of a hanger and tape in place, as shown.

4. Ask students to color the banners and cut them out. Then show students how to attach the banners to the hangers to complete their mobiles.

5. Hang the mobiles around the classroom when studying flying animals.

Flying Friends Mobile

© 1996 Troll Early Learning Activities

Flying Friends Mobile

FLYING
FRIENDS

© 1996 Troll Early Learning Activities

Elephants on Parade

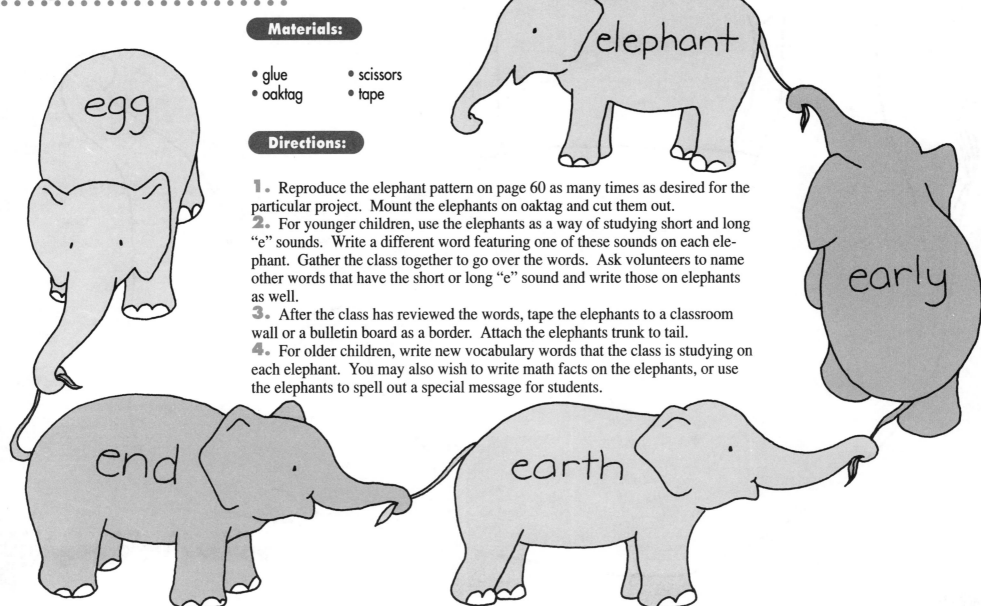

Materials:

- glue
- oaktag
- scissors
- tape

Directions:

1. Reproduce the elephant pattern on page 60 as many times as desired for the particular project. Mount the elephants on oaktag and cut them out.

2. For younger children, use the elephants as a way of studying short and long "e" sounds. Write a different word featuring one of these sounds on each elephant. Gather the class together to go over the words. Ask volunteers to name other words that have the short or long "e" sound and write those on elephants as well.

3. After the class has reviewed the words, tape the elephants to a classroom wall or a bulletin board as a border. Attach the elephants trunk to tail.

4. For older children, write new vocabulary words that the class is studying on each elephant. You may also wish to write math facts on the elephants, or use the elephants to spell out a special message for students.

Elephants on Parade

© 1996 Troll Early Learning Activities

Bug Off! Sugar Cookies

Materials:

- 1 1/4 cups powdered sugar
- 1/2 cup margarine or butter, softened
- 1/4 cup milk
- 1 egg, beaten
- 1/2 teaspoon vanilla
- 2 1/4 cups flour
- 2 teaspoons baking powder

- tubes of frosting
- large mixing bowl and spoon
- rolling pin
- plastic knives
- spatula
- cookie sheet
- cooling rack

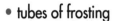

Directions:

1. Mix the powdered sugar, margarine or butter, milk, egg, and vanilla together in a large mixing bowl until creamy.
2. Gradually stir in the flour and baking powder.
3. Chill for three hours.
4. Give each child a small portion of the dough. Help each child roll out the dough on a floured surface.
5. Let students use plastic knives to cut out different bug shapes from the dough. For example, students may wish to make butterflies, ladybugs, or caterpillars with their dough.
6. Use a spatula to carefully place the cookies on a lightly greased cookie sheet.
7. Bake the cookies at 375°F for about eight minutes, or until the edges are slightly brown. Remove from the oven and place on a cooling rack.
8. After the cookies have cooled, let children use tubes of frosting to decorate their bugs.

Yields: 2-3 dozen cookies

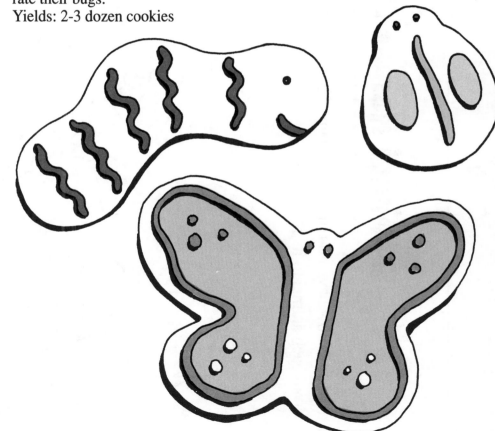

© 1996 Troll Early Learning Activities

Name _____

Animal Homes Mix-Up

The animals below have gotten all mixed up! Help them find their homes by drawing lines from each animal to its real home.

© 1996 Troll Early Learning Activities

Hidden Animal Babies

Fill in the missing letters of each animal baby's name.

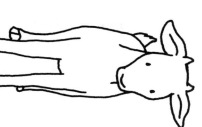

1. lion   c __ b

2. dog   p __ py

3. goose   __ os __ ing

4. hen   c __ ic __

5. goat   __ id

6. sheep   l __ b

7. horse   c __ lt

8. cow   c __ f

9. deer   __ a w __

10. frog   t __ d __ o l e

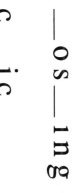

© 1996 Troll Early Learning Activities

Answers

page 14

Answers will vary.

page 45

1. F		6. T
2. T		7. F
3. F		8. F
4. T		9. T
5. T		10. T

page 46

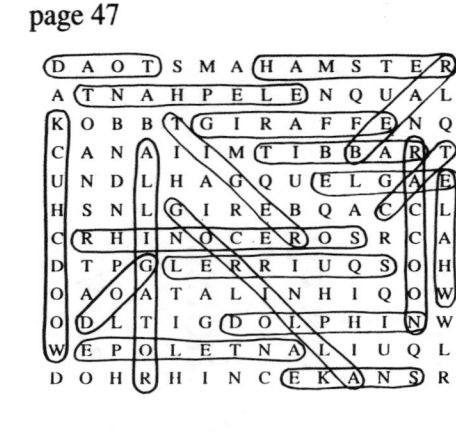

page 47

D A O T S M A H A M S T E R
A T N A H P E L E N Q U A L
K O B B T G I R A F F E N Q
C A N A I I M T I B B A R T
U N D L H A G Q U E L G A E
H S N L G I R E B Q A C C L
C R H I N O C E R O S R C A
D T P G L E R R I U Q S O H
O A O A T A L I N H I Q O W
O D L T I G D O L P H I N W
W E P O L E T N A L I U Q L
D O H R H I N C E K A N S R

page 62

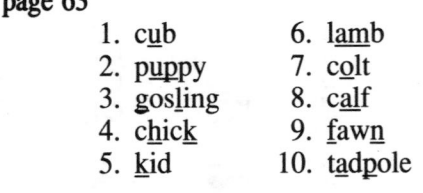

page 63

1. cub		6. lamb
2. puppy		7. colt
3. gosling		8. calf
4. chick		9. fawn
5. kid		10. tadpole

page 51

1. C		6. A
2. E		7. B
3. G		8. D
4. I		9. F
5. J		10. H

© 1996 Troll Early Learning Activities